GU01019089

1996   No. 323

MAGISTRATES' COURTS

Magistrates' Courts (Children (Northern Ireland) Order 1995) Rules (Northern Ireland) 1996

Made	*25th July 1996*
Coming into operation . .	*4th November 1996*

The Lord Chancellor, in exercise of the powers conferred on him by Article 13 of the Magistrates' Courts (Northern Ireland) Order 1981(**a**) and Article 71 and 165 of the Children (Northern Ireland) Order 1995(**b**) and all other powers enabling him in that behalf, on the advice of the Magistrates' Courts Rules Committee and after consultation with the Lord Chief Justice, hereby makes the following rules:—

Citation, commencement and interpretation

1.—(1) These Rules may be cited as the Magistrates' Courts (Children (Northern Ireland) Order 1995) Rules (Northern Ireland) 1996 and shall come into operation on 4th November 1996.

(2) Nothing in these rules shall affect any proceedings pending (within the meaning of paragraph 1 of Schedule 8 to the Children (Northern Ireland) Order 1995) immediately before these rules come into operation.

(3) In these rules unless the context otherwise requires—

"the Allocation Order" means the Children (Allocation of Proceedings) Order (Northern Ireland) 1996(**c**);

"application" means an application under or by virtue of the Order or under these Rules and "applicant" shall be construed accordingly;

"an Article 8 order" has the same meaning as in Article 8(2);

"Board" means a Health and Social Services Board;

"business day" means any day other than a Saturday, a Sunday, Christmas Day, Good Friday or a bank holiday which is, or is to be observed as, a bank holiday in Northern Ireland under the Banking and Financial Dealings Act 1971(**d**);

"child" means—

(*a*) subject to paragraph (*b*), a person under the age of 18 with respect to whom the proceedings are brought; and

---

(**a**)   S.I. 1981/1675 (N.I. 26)
(**b**)   S.I. 1995/755 (N.I. 2)
(**c**)   S.R. 1996 No. 300
(**d**)   1971 c. 80

(*b*) where the proceedings are under Schedule 1 also includes a person who has reached the age of 18;

"court" includes a family proceedings court to which proceedings are brought in accordance with the Allocation Order and a resident magistrate or member of a juvenile court panel in respect of the proceedings prescribed in rule 2(5)(*a*) and a resident magistrate in respect of the proceedings prescribed in rule 2(5)(*b*);

"directions appointment" means a hearing for directions under rule 15;

"document exchange" means any document exchange for the time being approved by the Lord Chancellor;

"file" means deposit with the clerk of petty sessions;

"guardian ad litem" means a guardian ad litem appointed under Article 60, of the child with respect to whom the proceedings are brought;

"leave" includes permission and approval;

"parental responsibility" has the same meaning as in Article 6;

"parties" in relation to any relevant proceedings means the respondents specified in column (iii) of Schedule 2 and the applicant;

"relevant proceedings" has the same meaning as in Article 165(3);

"specified proceedings" has the same meaning as in Article 60(6) and rule 2(2);

"the Order" means the Children (Northern Ireland) Order 1995 and an Article or Schedule referred to by number means the Article or Schedule so numbered in the Order;

"Trust" means a Health and Social Services Trust by whom functions are exercisable by virtue of an authorisation for the time being in operation under the Health and Personal Social Services (Northern Ireland) Order 1994(**a**);

"welfare officer" means a person who has been asked to prepare a welfare report under Article 4.

(4) Any reference to a form is a reference to a form in Schedule 1 to these rules and includes a reference to a form to the same effect with such variations as the circumstances might require.

(5) The Magistrates' Courts Rules (Northern Ireland) 1984(**b**) shall have effect subject to the provisions of these Rules.

Matters prescribed for the purposes of the Order

2.—(1) The parties to proceedings in which directions are given under Article 57(6) and any person named in such a direction, form the prescribed class for the purposes of Article 57(8)(*b*) (application to vary directions made with interim care or interim supervision order).

(2) The following proceedings are specified for the purposes of Article 60 in accordance with paragraph 6(i) thereof—

(**a**) S.I. 1994/429 (N.I. 2)
(**b**) S.R. 1984 No. 225

(i) Provision under which proceedings brought	(ii) Minimum number of days prior to hearing or directions appointment for service under rule 4(2)	(iii) Respondents	(iv) Persons to whom notice is to be given
		the application.	(i) every person whom the applicant believes to be a party to pending relevant proceedings in respect of the same child, and (ii) every person whom the applicant believes to be a parent without parental responsibility for the child.
Article 62(12)	2 days	As for "all applications" above.	Those of the persons referred to in Article 62(11)(*a*) to (*e*) who were not party to the application for the order which it is sought to have varied or discharged.
Article 44, 63(1), 63(9)(*b*), 64(3), 64(7), 67(9), 69(1), 178(1)	1 day	As for "all applications" above, and: in the case of an application under Article 63(9)(*b*)— (i) the parties to the application for the order in respect of which it is sought	Except for applications under Article 178(1), as for "all applications" above, and: in the case of an application under Article 63(1), every person whom the applicant believes to be a parent of the child;

(i)	(ii)	(iii)	(iv)
Provision under which proceedings brought	*Minimum number of days prior to hearing or directions appointment for service under rule 4(2)*	*Respondents*	*Persons to whom notice is to be given*
		to vary the directions; (ii) any person who was caring for the child prior to the making of the order, and (iii) any person whose contact with the child is affected by the direction which it is sought to have varied; in the case of an application under Article 69, the person whom the applicant alleges to have effected or to have been or to be responsible for the taking or keeping of the child.	in the case of an application under Article 63(9)(*b*)— (i) the authority in whose area the child is living, and (ii) any person whom the applicant believes to be affected by the direction which it is sought to have varied; in the case of an application under Article 178(1), the person referred to in Article 178(1) and any person preventing or likely to prevent such a person from exercising powers under enactments mentioned in paragraph (6) of that Article.

EXPLANATORY NOTE

(This note is not part of the Rules.)

These Rules provide for applications to a magistrates' court (including a family proceedings court) under the Children (Northern Ireland) Order 1995.

Printed in the United Kingdom for the
Controller of Her Majesty's Stationery Office
being the Officer appointed to print the
Measures of the Northern Ireland Assembly and
published by Her Majesty's Stationery Office

Dd. 310075. C12. 8/96. Gp. 130. 14567.

£9·40

(*a*) proceedings under Article 33(1);

(*b*) proceedings under Article 44;

(*c*) applications under Article 52(7);

(*d*) proceedings under paragraph 6(3) of Schedule 3.

(3) The applicant for an order that has been made under Article 62(1) and the persons referred to in Article 62(11) may, in any circumstances, apply under Article 62(12) for a child assessment order to be varied or discharged.

(4) The following persons form the prescribed class for the purposes of Article 63(9)(*b*) (application to vary directions)—

(*a*) the parties to the application in which it is sought to vary the directions;

(*b*) the guardian ad litem;

(*c*) the authority in whose area the child is ordinarily resident;

(*d*) any person who is named in the directions.

(5) Where, in accordance with the Allocation Order an application is required to be commenced in a family proceedings court the following proceedings are prescribed for the purposes of Article 165(2)(i)—

(*a*) proceedings on an ex parte application under Article 63; 67 and 69; and under rule 5 are proceedings with respect to which a resident magistrate or member of a juvenile court panel may discharge the functions of a court of summary jurisdiction; and

(*b*) proceedings in accordance with rule 3, 6, 7, 11, 15, 16, 17, 18, 19 and 20 are proceedings with respect to which a resident magistrate may discharge the functions of a court of summary jurisdiction.

Application for leave to commence proceedings

3.—(1) Where the leave of the court is required to bring any relevant proceedings, the person seeking leave shall file—

(*a*) an application for leave in Form C2; and

(*b*) a draft of the application in respect of which leave is sought in the appropriate form in Schedule 1 or where there is no such form, in writing, together with sufficient copies for one to be served on each respondent; and

(*c*) A draft summons in Form C1A.

(2) On considering a request for leave filed under paragraph (1), the court shall—

(*a*) grant the request whereupon the clerk of petty sessions shall issue a summons in Form C1A; or

(*b*) fix a date for a hearing of the request whereupon the clerk of petty sessions shall give such notice as the court directs to the person making the request and to such other persons as the court requires to be notified of the date so fixed.

Application

4.—(1) An application by way of complaint to a justice of the peace or clerk of petty sessions for an order under the Order shall be made in writing in Form C1 together with such of Forms C6 to C17 as is appropriate.

(2) Subject to paragraph (3) any summons issued in consequence of such an application shall be prepared by the applicant in Form C1A and shall be served on each respondent to the application along with a copy of the written application the minimum number of days prior to the date fixed for hearing as is specified in relation to that application in column (iii) of Schedule 2 to these rules.

(3) Where an applicant is also making an application for an order under the Domestic Proceedings (Northern Ireland) Order 1980(**a**) then any summons issued shall be in the appropriate form in the Magistrates' Courts (Domestic Proceedings) Rules 1996(**b**) and shall be prepared and served in accordance with those rules together with a copy of the written application referred to in paragraph (1).

(4) At the same time as complying with paragraph (2) or (3) notice of the proceedings in Form C2A shall also be given by the applicant to those persons set out in relation to the relevant class of proceedings in column (iv) of Schedule 2 to these rules.

Ex parte application

5.—(1) An application for—

(*a*) an Article 8 order;

(*b*) an emergency protection order under Article 63;

(*c*) an order or warrant under Article 67;

(*d*) a recovery order under Article 69; or

(*e*) a warrant under Article 178(2)

may with the leave of the court be made ex parte and in which case Article 77(2) of the Magistrates' Courts (Northern Ireland) Order 1981 (civil proceedings to be upon complaint) and rule 4 shall not apply.

(2) Where under paragraph (1) the leave of the court is granted the application may be made orally and the applicant shall within 48 hours of the making of the application—

(*a*) file a written copy of the application in Form C1 together with such of Forms C6 to C17 as is appropriate; and

(*b*) serve a copy of the application and any order on—

(i) the parties;

(ii) any person who has actual care of the child or had such care immediately prior to the making of the order; and

(iii) in the case of an order or warrant referred to in paragraph (1)(*b*) or (*c*) on the Board or Trust in whose area the child lives or was found.

(**a**) S.I. 1980/563 (N.I. 5)
(**b**) S.R. 1996 No.

(3) Where the court refuses to make an order on an ex parte application it may direct that the application be made inter partes.

Withdrawal of application

6.—(1) An application may be withdrawn only with leave of the court.

(2) Subject to paragraph (3) a person seeking leave to withdraw an application shall file and serve on the parties a written request for leave in Form C2 setting out the reasons for the request.

(3) The request under paragraph (2) may be made orally to the court if the parties and, if appointed, the guardian ad litem or the welfare officer are present.

(4) Upon receipt of a written request under paragraph (2), the court shall—

(*a*) if

   (i) the parties consent in writing,

   (ii) any guardian ad litem has had an opportunity to make representations, and

   (iii) the court thinks fit,

   grant the request; in which case the clerk of petty sessions shall notify the parties, and any guardian ad litem or welfare officer; or

(*b*) the court shall fix a date for the hearing of the request and the clerk of petty sessions shall give at least 7 days' notice to the parties, and any guardian ad litem or the welfare officer of the date so fixed.

Transfer of proceedings

7.—(1) Where in any relevant proceedings the court receives a request in writing from a party that the proceedings be transferred to a county court or the High Court in accordance with the Allocation Order the court shall issue an order or certificate in the appropriate form in Schedule 1 to these Rules granting or refusing the request.

(2) A copy of the order or certificate issued under paragraph (1) shall be sent by the clerk of petty sessions—

(*a*) to the parties,

(*b*) to any guardian ad litem, and

(*c*) to the chief clerk of the county court or the Master (Probate and Matrimonial) or the Master (Care and Protection) of the High Court as the case may be.

Parties

8.—(1) The respondents to relevant proceedings shall be those persons set out in the relevant entry in column (iii) of Schedule 2 to these rules.

(2) In any relevant proceedings a person may file a request in Form C2 that he or another person—

(*a*) be joined as a party, or

(*b*) cease to be a party.

5

(3) On considering a request under paragraph (2) the court shall, subject to paragraph (4)—

(a) grant it without a hearing or representations, save that this shall be done only in the case of a request under paragraph (2)(a), whereupon the clerk of petty sessions shall inform in writing the parties and the person making the request of that decision, or

(b) order that a date be fixed for the consideration of the request, whereupon the clerk of petty sessions shall give notice in writing of the date so fixed, together with a copy of the request—

(i) in the case of a request under paragraph (2)(a), to the applicant and the person to be joined if he is not also the applicant, and

(ii) in the case of a request under paragraph (2)(b), to the parties, or

(c) invite the parties or any of them to make written representations, within a specified period, as to whether the request should be granted; and upon the expiry of the period the court shall act in accordance with sub-paragraph (a) or (b).

(4) Where a person with parental responsibility requests that he be joined under paragraph (2)(a), the court shall grant his request.

(5) In any relevant proceedings the court may direct—

(a) that a person who would not otherwise be a respondent under these Rules be joined as a party to the proceedings, or

(b) that a party to the proceedings cease to be a party.

Service

9.—(1) Rule 11 of the Magistrates' Courts Rules (Northern Ireland) 1984 shall apply to the service of a summons under these Rules.

(2) Service of any other document under these Rules may be effected—

(a) if the person to be served is not known by the person serving to be acting by solicitor—

(i) by delivering it to him personally, or

(ii) by delivering it at, or by sending it by first class post to, his residence or his last known residence, or

(b) if the person to be served is known by the person serving to be acting by solicitor—

(i) by delivering the document at, or sending it by first class post to, the solicitor's address for service,

(ii) where the solicitor's address for service includes a numbered box at a document exchange, by leaving the document at that document exchange or at a document exchange which transmits documents on every business day to that document exchange, or

(iii) by sending a legible copy of the document by facsimile transmission to the solicitor's office.

(3) In this rule, "first class post" means first class post which has been pre-paid or in respect of which pre-payment is not required.

(4) Where a child who is a party to any relevant proceedings is required by these rules to serve a document, service shall be effected by—

(a) the solicitor acting for the child,

(b) where there is no such solicitor, the guardian ad litem, or

(c) where there is neither such a solicitor nor a guardian ad litem, the clerk of petty sessions.

(5) Service of any document on a child shall, subject to any direction of the court, be effected by service on—

(a) the solicitor acting for the child,

(b) where there is no such solicitor, the guardian ad litem, or

(c) where there is neither such a solicitor nor a guardian ad litem, with leave of the court, the child.

(6) Where the court refuses leave under paragraph (5)(c), a direction shall be given under paragraph (8).

(7) A document shall, unless the contrary is proved, be deemed to have been served—

(a) in the case of service by first class post, on the second business day after posting, and

(b) in the case of service in accordance with paragraph (1)(b)(ii), on the second business day after the day on which it is left at the document exchange.

(8) In any relevant proceedings, where these rules require a document to be served, the court may, without prejudice to any power under rule 15, direct that—

(a) the requirement shall not apply;

(b) the time specified by the rules for complying with the requirement shall be abridged to such extent as may be specified in the direction;

(c) service shall be effected in such manner as may be specified in the direction.

Acknowledgement of application

10. Within 14 days of the service of a summons on an application for an Article 8 order or an application under Schedule 1 each respondent shall file and serve on the parties an acknowledgement in Form C4.

Appointment of guardian ad litem

11.—(1) As soon as practicable after the commencement of specified proceedings the court shall appoint a guardian ad litem unless the court considers that such an appointment is not necessary to safeguard the interests of the child.

(2) At any stage in specified proceedings a party may apply, without notice to the other parties unless the court otherwise directs, for the appointment of a guardian ad litem.

(3) The court shall grant an application under paragraph (2) unless it is considered that such an appointment is not necessary to safeguard the interests

of the child, in which case reasons shall be given; and a note of such reasons shall be taken by the clerk of petty sessions.

(4) At any stage in specified proceedings the court may appoint a guardian ad litem even though no application is made for such an appointment.

(5) The clerk of petty sessions shall, as soon as practicable, notify the parties and any welfare officer in Form C41 of an appointment under this rule or, as the case may be, of a decision not to make such an appointment.

(6) Upon the appointment of a guardian ad litem the clerk of petty sessions shall, as soon as practicable, notify him of the appointment in Form C41 and serve on him copies of the application and of documents filed under rule 18(1).

(7) A guardian ad litem appointed from a panel established by regulations made under Article 60(7) shall not—

(a) be a member, officer or servant of a Board or Trust which, or an authorised person (within the meaning of Article 49(2)) who, is a party to the proceedings;

(b) be, or have been, a member, officer or servant of a Board or Trust voluntary organisation (within the meaning of Article 74(1)) who has been directly concerned in that capacity in arrangements relating to the care, accommodation or welfare of the child during the five years prior to the commencement of the proceedings;

(c) be a serving probation officer (except that a probation officer who has not in that capacity been previously concerned with the child or his family and who is employed part-time may, when not engaged in his duties as a probation officer, act as a guardian ad litem).

(8) When appointing a guardian ad litem, the court may give consideration to appointing of anyone who has previously acted as guardian ad litem of the same child.

(9) The appointment of a guardian ad litem under this rule shall continue for such time as is specified in the appointment or until terminated by the court.

(10) When terminating an appointment in accordance with paragraph (9), the court shall give reasons in writing for so doing, and the clerk of petty sessions shall notify the parties, any welfare officer and the guardian ad litem of the termination in Form C41.

Powers and duties of guardian ad litem

12.—(1) In carrying out his duty under Article 60(2) the guardian at litem shall have regard to the principle set out in Article 3(2) and the matters set out in Article 3(3)(a) to (f) as if for the word 'court' in that Article there were substituted the words 'guardian ad litem'.

(2) The guardian ad litem shall—

(a) appoint a solicitor to represent the child, unless such a solicitor has already been appointed, and (*b*) give such advice to the child as is appropriate having regard to his understanding and, subject to rule 13(1)(*a*), instruct the solicitor representing the child on all matters relevant to the interests of the child, including possibilities for appeal, arising in the course of the proceedings.

(3) Where it appears to the guardian ad litem that the child—

(*a*) is instructing his solicitor direct, or

(*b*) intends to, and is capable of, conducting the proceedings on his own behalf,

he shall so inform the court and thereafter—

(i) shall perform all of his duties set out in this rule, other than duties under paragraph (2)(*a*) and such other duties as the court may direct,

(ii) shall take such part in the proceedings as the court may direct, and

(iii) may, with leave of the court, have legal representation in his conduct of those duties.

(4) The guardian ad litem shall, unless excused by the court, attend all directions appointments in, and hearings of, the proceedings and shall advise the court on the following matters—

(*a*) whether the child is of sufficient understanding for any purpose including the child's refusal to submit to a medical or psychiatric examination or other assessment that the court has power to require, direct or order;

(*b*) the wishes of a child in respect of any matter relevant to the proceedings, including his attendance at court;

(*c*) the appropriate forum for the proceedings;

(*d*) the appropriate timing of the proceedings or any part of them;

(*e*) the options available to it in respect of the child and the suitability of each such option including what order should be made in determining the application;

(*f*) any other matter concerning which the court seeks his advice or concerning which he considers that the court should be informed.

(5) The advice given under paragraph (4) may, subject to any order of the court, be given orally or in writing; and if the advice be given orally, a note of it shall be taken by the court.

(6) The guardian ad litem shall, where practicable, notify any person whose joinder as a party to those proceedings would be likely, in the guardian ad litem's opinion, to safeguard the interests of the child, of that person's right to apply to be joined under rule (8)(2) and shall inform the court—

(*a*) of any such notification given,

(*b*) of anyone whom he attempted to notify under this paragraph but was unable to contact, and

(*c*) of anyone whom he believes may wish to be joined to the proceedings.

(7) The guardian ad litem shall, unless the court otherwise directs, not less than 7 days before the date fixed for the final hearing of the proceedings,

file a written report advising on the interests of the child; and the clerk of petty sessions shall, as soon as practicable, serve a copy of the report on the parties.

(8) The guardian ad litem shall serve and accept service of documents on behalf of the child in accordance with rule 9(4)(*b*) and (5)(*b*) and, where the child has not himself been served, and has sufficient understanding, advise the child of the contents of any documents so served.

(9) The guardian ad litem shall make such investigations as may be necessary for him to carry out his duties and shall, in particular—

(*a*) contact or seek to interview such persons as he thinks appropriate or as the court directs,

(*b*) if he inspects records of the kinds referred to in Article 61, bring to the attention of the court, and such other persons as the court may direct, all such records and documents which may, in his opinion, assist in the proper determination of the proceedings, and

(*c*) obtain such professional assistance as is available to him which he thinks appropriate or which the court directs him to obtain.

(10) In addition to his duties under other paragraphs of this rule, the guardian ad litem shall provide to the court such other assistance as may be required.

(11) A party may question the guardian ad litem about oral or written advice tendered by him to the court under this rule.

Solicitor for child

13.—(1) A solicitor appointed under Article 60(3) or in accordance with rule 12(2)(*a*) shall represent the child—

(*a*) in accordance with instructions received from the guardian ad litem (unless the solicitor considers, having taken into account the views of the guardian ad litem and any direction of the court under rule 12(3), that the child wishes to give instructions which conflict with those of the guardian ad litem and that he is able, having regard to his understanding, to give such instructions on his own behalf in which case he shall conduct the proceedings in accordance with instructions received from the child), or

(*b*) where no guardian ad litem has been appointed for the child and the condition in Article 60(4)(*b*) is satisfied, in accordance with instructions received from the child, or

(*c*) in default of instructions under (*a*) or (*b*), in furtherance of the best interests of the child.

(2) A solicitor appointed under Article 60(3) or in accordance with rule 12(2)(*a*) shall serve and accept service of documents on behalf of the child in accordance with rule 9(4)(*a*) and (5)(*a*) and, where the child has not himself been served and has sufficient understanding, advise the child of the contents of any documents so served.

(3) Where the child wishes an appointment of a solicitor under Article 60(3) or in accordance with rule 12(2)(*a*) to be terminated, he may apply to the court for an order terminating the appointment; and the solicitor and the guardian ad litem shall be given an opportunity to make representations.

(4) Where the guardian ad litem wishes an appointment of a solicitor under Article 60(3) to be terminated, he may apply to the court for an order terminating the appointment; and the solicitor and, if he is of sufficient understanding, the child, shall be given an opportunity to make representations.

(5) When terminating an appointment in accordance with paragraph (3) or (4), the court shall give reasons in writing for so doing and the clerk of petty sessions shall notify the solicitor, the parties, the guardian ad litem and any welfare officer of the termination in Form C42.

Welfare Officer

14.—(1) Where the court has directed that a written report be made by a welfare officer, the report shall be filed at or by such time as the court directs or, in the absence of such a direction, at least 14 days before a relevant hearing; and the clerk of petty sessions shall, as soon as practicable, serve a copy of the report on the parties and any guardian ad litem.

(2) In paragraph (1), a hearing is relevant if the clerk of petty sessions has given the welfare officer notice that his report is to be considered at it.

(3) After the filing of a written report by a welfare officer, the court may direct that the welfare officer attend any hearing at which the report is to be considered; and

(*a*) except where such a direction is given at a hearing attended by the welfare officer, the clerk of petty sessions shall inform the welfare officer of the direction; and

(*b*) at the hearing at which the report is considered any party may question the welfare officer about his report.

(4) This rule is without prejudice to the court's power to give directions under rule 15.

Directions

15.—(1) In this rule 'party' includes the guardian ad litem and where a request or direction concerns a report under Article 4, the welfare officer.

(2) In any relevant proceedings the court may, subject to paragraph (4), give, vary or revoke directions for the conduct of the proceedings, including—

(*a*) the timetable for the proceedings;

(*b*) varying the time within which or by which an act is required, by these rules, to be done;

(*c*) the attendance of the child;

(*d*) the appointment of a guardian ad litem whether under Article 60 or otherwise, or of a solicitor under Article 60(3);

(*e*) the service of documents;

(*f*) the submission of evidence including experts' reports;

(*g*) the preparation of welfare reports under Article 4;

(*h*) the transfer of the proceedings to another court in accordance with the Allocation Order;

(*i*) consolidation with other proceedings;

and the clerk of petty sessions shall, on receipt of an application, or where proceedings have been transferred to his court, refer the application to the court to consider whether such directions need to be given.

(3) Where a direction is given under paragraph (2)(*h*), an order or certificate shall be issued in the appropriate form in Schedule 1 to these rules and the clerk of petty sessions shall follow the procedure set out in rule 7(2).

(4) Directions under paragraph (2) may be given, varied or revoked either—

(*a*) of the court's own motion and having given the parties notice in Form C3 of the intention to do so and an opportunity to attend and be heard or to make written representations,

(*b*) on the written request in Form C2 of a party specifying the direction which is sought, filed and served on the other parties, or

(*c*) on the written request in Form C2 of a party specifying the direction which is sought, to which the other parties consent and which they or their representatives have signed.

(5) In an urgent case, the request under paragraph (4)(*b*) may, with the leave of the court, be made—

(*a*) orally,

(*b*) without notice to the parties, or

(*c*) both as in sub-paragraph (*a*) and as in sub-paragraph (*b*).

(6) On receipt of a request under paragraph (4)(*b*) the clerk of petty sessions shall fix a date for the hearing of the request and give not less than 2 days' notice in Form C3 to the parties of the date so fixed.

(7) On considering a request under paragraph (4)(*c*) the court shall either—

(*a*) grant the request, whereupon the clerk of petty sessions shall inform the parties of the decision, or

(*b*) fix a date for the hearing of the request, whereupon the clerk of petty sessions shall give not less than 2 days' notice in Form C3 to the parties of the date so fixed.

(8) A party may request, in accordance with paragraph 4(*b*) or (*c*), that an order be made under Article 11(3) or, if he is entitled to apply for such an order, under Article 57(1), and paragraphs (5), (6) and (7) shall apply accordingly.

(9) Where, in any relevant proceedings, the court has power to make an order of its own motion, the power to give directions under paragraph (2) shall apply.

(10) Directions of a court which are still in force immediately prior to the transfer of relevant proceedings to another court shall continue to apply following the transfer, subject to any changes of terminology which are required to apply those directions to the court to which the proceedings are transferred, unless varied or discharged by directions under paragraph (2).

(11) The court shall record the giving, variation or revocation of a direction under this rule in Form C18 and the clerk of petty sessions shall serve, as soon as practicable, a copy of the form on any party who was not present at the giving, variation or revocation.

Timing of proceedings

16. At the—

(*a*) transfer of relevant proceedings to a family proceedings court in accordance with Article 10 or 11 of the Allocation Order, or

(*b*) postponement or adjournment of any hearing or directions appointment,

the court shall—

(i) fix a date upon which the proceedings shall next come before the court, which date shall where paragraph (*a*) applies, be as soon as possible after the transfer; and

(ii) give notice to the parties and any guardian ad litem or welfare officer of the date so fixed.

Attendance at directions appointment and hearing

17.—(1) Subject to paragraph (2), a party shall attend a directions appointment of which he has been given notice in accordance with rule 15(4) unless the court otherwise directs.

(2) Relevant proceedings shall take place in the absence of any party including the child if—

(*a*) the court considers it in the interests of the child, having regard to the matters to be discussed or the evidence likely to be given, and

(*b*) the party is represented by a guardian ad litem or solicitor;

and when considering the interests of the child under sub-paragraph (*a*) the court shall give the guardian ad litem, solicitor for the child and, if he is of sufficient understanding, the child, an opportunity to make representations.

(3) Subject to paragraph (4) below, where at the time and place appointed for a hearing or directions appointment the applicant appears but one or more of the respondents do not, the court may proceed with the hearing or appointment.

(4) The court shall not begin to hear an application in the absence of a respondent unless—

(*a*) it is proved to the satisfaction of the court that he received reasonable notice of the date of the hearing; or

(*b*) the court is satisfied that the circumstances of the case justify proceeding with the hearing.

(5) Where, at the time and place appointed for a hearing or directions appointment, one or more respondents appear but the applicant does not, the court may refuse the application or, if sufficient evidence has previously been received, proceed in the absence of the applicant.

(6) Where at the time and place appointed for a hearing or directions appointment neither the applicant nor any respondent appears, the court may refuse the application.

(7) If the court considers it expedient in the interests of the child, it shall hear any relevant proceedings in private when only the officers of the court, the parties, their legal representatives and such other persons as specified by the court may attend.

Evidence

18.—(1) Subject to paragraphs (4) and (5) in any relevant proceedings a party shall file and serve on the other parties, any welfare officer and any guardian ad litem of whose appointment he has been given notice under rule 11(5)—

(*a*) written statements in Form C46 of the substance of the oral evidence which the party intends to adduce at a hearing of, or a directions appointment in, those proceedings,

(*b*) copies of any documents, including, subject to rule 19(3), experts' reports, upon which the party intends to rely, at a hearing of, or a directions appointment in, those proceedings,

at or by such time as the court directs or, in the absence of a direction, before the hearing or appointment.

(2) A party may, subject to any direction of the court about the timing of statements under this rule, file and serve on the parties a statement which is supplementary to a statement served under paragraph (1).

(3) At a hearing or directions appointment a party may not, without the leave of the court—

(*a*) adduce evidence, or

(*b*) seek to rely on a document,

in respect of which he has failed to comply with the requirements of paragraph (1).

(4) In proceedings for an Article 8 order a party shall—

(*a*) neither file nor serve any document other than as required or authorised by these Rules, and

(*b*) in completing a form prescribed by these Rules, neither give information, nor make a statement, which is not required or authorised by that form,

without the leave of the court.

(5) In proceedings for an Article 8 order, no statement or copy may be filed under paragraph (1) unless the court otherwise directs.

14

Expert evidence: examination of child

19.—(1) No person may, without the leave of the court, cause a child to be medically or psychiatrically examined, or otherwise assessed, for the purpose of the preparation of expert evidence for use in the proceedings.

(2) An application for leave under paragraph (1) shall be made in Form C2 and shall, unless the court otherwise directs, be served on all the parties to the proceedings and on any guardian ad litem.

(3) Where the leave of the court has not been given under paragraph (1), no evidence arising out of an examination or assessment to which that paragraph applies may be adduced without the leave of the court.

Amendment

20.—(1) Subject to rule 18(2), a document which has been filed or served in any relevant proceedings may not be amended without the leave of the court which shall, unless the court otherwise directs, be requested in writing.

(2) On considering a request for leave to amend a document the court shall either—

(*a*) grant the request, whereupon the clerk of petty sessions shall inform the person making the request of that decision, or

(*b*) invite the parties or any of them to make representations, within a specified period, as to whether such an order should be made.

(3) A person amending a document shall file it with the clerk of petty sessions and serve it on those persons on whom it was served prior to amendment; and the amendments shall be identified.

Hearing

21.—(1) Before the hearing the resident magistrate and any members of the juvenile court panel who will be dealing with the case shall read any documents which have been filed under rule 18.

(2) Unless the court otherwise directs at a hearing of, or directions appointment in, relevant proceedings the parties and the guardian ad litem shall adduce their evidence in the following order—

(*a*) the applicant,

(*b*) any party with parental responsibility for the child,

(*c*) other respondents,

(*d*) the guardian ad litem,

(*e*) the child if he is a party to the proceedings and there is no guardian ad litem.

(3) After the final hearing of relevant proceedings, the court shall make its decision as soon as is practicable.

(4) Before the court makes an order or refuses an application the resident magistrate shall record in writing—

(*a*) the names of any members of the juvenile court panel who heard the case with him;

(*b*) the reasons for the court's decision and any findings of fact.

(5) When making an order or when refusing an application the resident magistrate shall—

   (*a*) where the court has made a finding of fact state such finding and complete Form C19; and

   (*b*) state the reasons for the court's decision.

(6) After the court announces its decision, the clerk of petty sessions shall, subject to rule 5(2)(*b*), as soon as practicable serve a copy of the order in the prescribed form in Schedule 1 to these rules on the parties to the proceedings and or any person with whom the child is living.

Costs

22.—(1) In any relevant proceedings, the court may, at any time during the proceedings in that court, make an order that a party pay the whole or any part of the costs of any other party.

(2) A party against whom the court is considering making a costs order shall have an opportunity to make representations as to why the order should not be made.

Confidentiality of documents

23.—(1) Subject to paragraphs (2) and (3) no document, other than a record of an order, held by the court and relating to relevant proceedings shall be disclosed, other than to—

   (*a*) a party,

   (*b*) the legal representative of a party,

   (*c*) the guardian ad litem,

   (*d*) the Legal Aid Department, or

   (*e*) a welfare officer

without the leave of the court.

(2) Where the Department of Health and Social Services requires a person mentioned in regulation 2(2) or (3) of the Child Support (Information, Evidence and Disclosure) Regulations (Northern Ireland) 1992(**a**) to furnish information or evidence for a purpose mentioned in regulation 3(1) of those Regulations, nothing in paragraph (1) shall prevent that person from furnishing the information or evidence sought or to require him to seek the leave of the court before doing so.

(3) Nothing in paragraph (1) shall prevent the notification by the court of a direction under Article 56(1) to the authority concerned.

Disclosure of address

24.—(1) Nothing in these rules shall be construed as requiring any party to reveal the address of their private residence or that of any child except by order of the court.

(**a**) S.R. 1992 No. 339

(2) Where a party declines to reveal an address in reliance upon paragraph (1) he shall give notice of that address to the court in Form C5 and that address shall not be revealed to any person except by order of the court.

Notification of consent

25. Consent for the purposes of—

(*a*) Article 16(3), or

(*b*) Article 33(1)

may be given either orally in court or in writing signed by the person giving his consent.

Secure accommodation

26. In proceedings under Article 44 the clerk of petty sessions shall, if practicable, arrange for copies of all written reports before the court to be made available before the hearing to—

(*a*) the applicant,

(*b*) the parent or guardian of the child,

(*c*) any legal representative of the child,

(*d*) the guardian ad litem, and

(*e*) the child, unless the court otherwise directs;

and copies of such reports may, if the court considers it desirable, be shown to any person who is entitled to notice of the proceedings in accordance with these Rules.

Investigation under Article 56

27.—(1) On giving a direction under Article 56 the court shall adjourn the proceedings and the clerk of petty sessions shall record the direction in Form C35.

(2) A copy of the direction recorded under paragraph (1) shall, as soon as practicable after the direction is given be served by the clerk of petty sessions on the parties to the proceedings in which the direction is given and, where the appropriate authority is not a party, on that authority.

(3) When serving the copy of the direction on the appropriate authority the clerk of petty sessions shall also serve copies of such of the documentary evidence which has been or is to be adduced in the proceedings as the court may direct.

(4) Where an authority informs the court of any of the matters set out in Article 56(3)(*a*) to (*c*) it shall do so in writing.

Appeals to a family proceedings court

28.—(1) An appeal to a family proceedings court under—

(*a*) Article 113,

(*b*) Article 131(6), or

(*c*) Article 145

shall be brought by notice in Form C46 and shall be signed by the appellant or his legal representative.

(2) The notice of appeal shall be accompanied by any copy of the decision or determination appealed against.

(3) An appeal under Article 131(6) may only be brought within 21 days from the date of the step to which the appeal relates.

(4) The clerk of petty sessions shall fix a date for the hearing of the appeal and shall give at least seven days' notice of the date so fixed to the parties.

Contribution orders

29.—(1) An application for a contribution order under Article 41(1) shall be accompanied by a copy of the contribution notice served in accordance with Article 40(1) and a copy of any notice served by the contributor under Article 40(8).

(2) Where an authority notifies the court of an agreement reached under Article 41(6) it shall do so in writing through the clerk of petty sessions.

(3) An application for the variation or revocation of a contribution order under Article 41(8) shall be accompanied by a copy of the contribution order which it is sought to vary or revoke.

Direction to an education and library board

30.—(1) For the purpose of paragraph 6 of Schedule 13 to the Education and Libraries (Northern Ireland) Order 1986(**a**) a direction to an education and libraries board to apply for an education supervision order shall be in Form C35A.

(2) Where, following such a direction the education and library board informs the court that they have decided not to apply for an education supervision order, they shall do so in writing.

Dated 25th July 1996.   *Mackay of Clashfern*, C.

(**a**)   S.I. 1986/594 (N.I. 3)

18

FORMS

FORM C1

APPLICATION FOR AN ORDER

Children (Northern Ireland) Order 1995

*Magistrates' Courts (Children (Northern Ireland) Order 1995)
Rules (Northern Ireland) 1996*

---

of

            Applicant

of

           Respondent

[Petty Sessions District of]

[Family Proceedings Court at]

County Court Division of

---

1 About you (the applicant)

State
- *your title, full name, address, telephone number, date of birth and relationship to each child above*
- *your solicitor's name, address, reference, telephone, FAX and DX numbers.*

2 The child(ren) and the order(s) you are applying for

For each child state
- *the full name, date of birth and sex*
- *the type of order(s) you are applying for (for example, residence order, contact order, supervision order).*

3 Other cases which concern the child(ren)

If there have ever been, or there are pending, any court cases (including cases outside Northern Ireland) which concern

- *a child whose name you have put in paragraph 2*
- *a full, half or step brother or sister of a child whose name you have put in paragraph 2*
- *a person in this case who is or has been, involved in caring for a child whose name you have put in paragraph 2*

attach a copy of the relevant order and give

- *the name of the court*
- *the name and panel address (if known) of the guardian ad litem, if appointed*
- *the name and contact address (if known) of the solicitor appointed for the child(ren).*

4 The respondent(s)

Schedule 2

For each respondent state
- *the title, full name and address*
- *the date of birth (if known) or the age*
- *the relationship to each child.*

5 Others to whom notice is to be given

Schedule 2

For each person state
- *the title, full name and address*
- *the date of birth (if known) or age*
- *the relationship to each child.*

6 The care of the child(ren)

For each child in paragraph 2 state
- *the child's current address and how long the child has lived there*
- *whether it is the child's usual address and who cares for the child there*
- *the child's relationship to the other children (if any).*

7 Social Services

For each child in paragraph 2 state
- *whether the child is known to the Social Services.*

  If so, give the name of the social worker and the address of the Social Services department.
- *whether the child is, or has been, on the Child Protection Register. If so, give the date of registration.*

8 The education and health of the child(ren)

For each child state
- *the name of the school, college or place of training which the child attends*
- *whether the child is in good health. Give details of any serious disabilities or ill-health*
- *whether the child has any special needs.*

9 The parents of the child(ren)

For each child state
- *the full name of the child's mother and father*
- *whether the parents are, or have been, married to each other*
- *whether the parents live together. If so, where*
- *whether, to your knowledge, either of the parents have been involved in any court case concerning a child. If so, give the date and the name of the court.*

10 The family of the child(ren) (other children)

For any other child not already mentioned in the family (for example, a brother or a half sister) state
- *the full name and address*
- *the date of birth (if known) or age*
- *the relationship of the child to you.*

11 Other adults

State
- *the full name of any other adults (for example, lodgers) who live at the same address as any child named in paragraph 2*
- *whether they live there all the time*
- *whether, to your knowledge the adult has been involved in any court case concerning a child. If so, give the date and the name of the court.*

12 Your reason(s) for applying and any plans for the child(ren)

State briefly your reasons for applying and what you want the court to order

- ***Do not** give a full statement if you are applying for an order under Article 8 of the Children (Northern Ireland) Order 1995. You may be asked to provide a full statement later.*
- ***Do not** complete this section if this form is accompanied by a prescribed supplement.*

13 At the court

State
- *whether you will need an interpreter at court (parties are responsible for providing their own). If so, specify the language.*
- *whether disabled facilities will be needed at court.*

Signed
(Applicant)

Date

SUMMONS TO RESPONDENT ON
AN APPLICATION UNDER THE
CHILDREN (NORTHERN IRELAND) ORDER 1995

of   Family Proceedings Court at

     Applicant

of   County Court Division of

     Respondent

Whereas an application a copy of which is attached has been made under Article
of the above Order.

THIS IS TO COMMAND YOU to appear as respondent on the hearing of the said
application at   on the   day of   19   at   o'clock
before the Family Proceedings Court sitting at

Dated this   day of   19   .

                        Justice of the Peace
                        [or Clerk of Petty Sessions]

APPLICATION

- for leave to commence proceedings

  Magistrates' Courts (Children (Northern Ireland) Order 1995) Rules (Northern Ireland) 1996: Rule 3

- for an order or directions in existing family proceedings

  Children (Northern Ireland) Order 1995

- to be joined as, or cease to be, a party in existing family proceedings

  Magistrates' Courts (Children (Northern Ireland) Order 1995) Rules (Northern Ireland) 1996: Rule 8

[PETTY SESSIONS DISTRICT OF]

[FAMILY PROCEEDINGS COURT AT]

of
Applicant

COUNTY COURT DIVISION OF

of
Respondent

1 About you (the person making this application)

State
- *your title, full name, address, telephone number, date of birth and relationship to each child above*
- *your solicitor's name, address, reference, telephone, FAX and DX numbers*
- *if you are already a party to the case, give your description*

  (for example, applicant, respondent or other).

2 The order(s) or direction(s) you are applying for

State for each child
- *the full name, date of birth and sex*
- *the type of order(s) you are applying for (for example, residence order, contact order, supervision order).*

3 Persons to be served with this application

For each respondent to this application state the title, full name and address.

4 Your reason(s) for applying and any plans for the child(ren)

State briefly your reasons for applying.

Do not *give a full statement if you are applying for an order under Article 8 Children (Northern Ireland) Order 1995.*

You may be asked to provide a full statement later.

Signed
(Applicant)

Date

FORM C2A

NOTICE TO NON-PARTIES OF
PROCEEDINGS
Children (Northern Ireland) Order 1995

To	of
	[FAMILY PROCEEDINGS COURT AT]
of	
Applicant	[PETTY SESSIONS DISTRICT OF]
of	
Respondent	COUNTY COURT DIVISION OF

The applicant has applied for an order under Article   of the Children (Northern Ireland) Order 1995 in respect of the following child(ren)

The court will consider the application at

on

at   [am]   ·   [pm]

The hearing is estimated to last

What to do next

You have been named in the application. Please read the notes overleaf.

If you go to court please take this Notice with you and show it to a court official.

About this Notice

Note 1 **You do not have the right to take part in the proceedings, at present.**

If you want to take part (become a party to the proceedings) you must apply to the court on Form C2.

You can obtain Form C2 from a court office. The application must be made to the court sending you this notice.

Note 2 For legal advice go to a solicitor or an advice agency.

Some solicitors specialise in court proceedings which involve children. You can obtain the address of a solicitor or an advice agency from the Yellow Pages or the Law Society.

A solicitor or an advice agency will be able to tell you whether you may be eligible for legal aid.

NOTICE TO PARTIES OF
DIRECTIONS APPOINTMENT

Children (Northern Ireland) Order 1995

of	[FAMILY PROCEEDINGS COURT AT]
Applicant	[PETTY SESSIONS DISTRICT OF]
of	
Respondent	COUNTY COURT DIVISION OF

The Applicant has applied to the court for an order under Article   of the
Children (Northern Ireland) Order 1995 in respect of the following child[ren]:

Directions Appointment

You should attend when the court considers the directions giving/varying/revocation

on

at   [am]   [pm]

The hearing is estimated to last

What to do next

When you go to court please take this Notice with you and show it to a court official.

About this Notice

Note 1	**At the directions appointment**	you will be able to tell the court about any special needs or circumstances of the child(ren).
Note 2	**For legal advice**	go to a solicitor or an advice agency.
		Some solicitors specialise in court proceedings which involve children. You can obtain the address of a solicitor or an advice agency from the Yellow Pages or the Law Society.
		A solicitor or an advice agency will be able to tell you whether you may be eligible for legal aid.
Note 3	**If you want to apply for an order**	in respect of any of the children named on the Notice, fill in Form C1.
		You can obtain the form from a court office. The application must be made to the court sending you this notice.

ACKNOWLEDGEMENT

The Court

The full name of the applicant

The full name(s) of the child(ren)

Date of [Hearing] [Directions Appointment]

What you (the person receiving this form) should do
- Answer the questions overleaf.
- If you need more space for an answer use a separate sheet of paper. please put your full name and case number at the top.
- If the applicant has asked the court to order you to make a payment for a child you must also fill in a Statement of Means (Form C7A). You can obtain this form from a court office if one has not been enclosed with the papers served on you.
- When you have answered the questions make copies of both sides of this form. You will need a copy for the applicant, and each party named in Part 4 of Form C1.
- Post, or hand, a copy to the applicant and to each party. Then post, or take, this form, and the Statement of Means if you filled one in, to the court at the address below.

You must do this **within 14 days** of the date when you were served with the summons **or** of the postmark on the envelope if the Notice of Proceedings was posted to you.

To be completed by the court	
	The court office is open
	from am to pm
	on Mondays to Fridays
1 About you	Full name
	Date of birth
	Address
Please give a daytime telephone number if you can.	Telephone Number

26

2 About your solicitor

If you do not have a solicitor put **None.** *(But see note 3 on the Notice of Proceedings which was served on you).*

Name

Address

Telephone
Number

FAX Number

DX Number

3 Address to which letters and other papers should be sent.

4 The application was received on:

5 Do you oppose the application?

6 Do you intend to apply to the court for an order?

7 Will you use an interpreter at court?

If Yes state the language into which the interpreter will translate.

Note: If you require an interpreter you must bring your own.

Signed
(Respondent)

Date

FORM C5

CONFIDENTIAL ADDRESS

*Magistrates' Courts (Children Order (Northern Ireland) 1995) Rules
(Northern Ireland) 1996*

The court

Case number

The full name(s) of the child(ren)

Child(ren)'s number(s)

Your full name

The omitted address

*This form is to be used by any party in Family Proceedings who does not wish to
reveal the address of their private residence or that of any child. This address will
not be revealed to any person save by order of the court. State that address.*

FORM C6

SUPPLEMENT FOR AN APPLICATION
CONCERNING THE REGISTRATION OF A CHILD-MINDER
OR PROVIDER OF DAY CARE

Article 129 Children (Northern Ireland) Order 1995

FAMILY PROCEEDINGS COURT AT

of

Applicant

of

Respondent

COUNTY COURT DIVISION OF

---

1 About you (the applicant)

State • the name of your Board or Trust, address, reference, telephone, FAX and DX numbers

• your solicitor's name, address, reference, telephone, FAX and DX numbers.

2 About the respondent (the child-minder or provider of day care)

State • the full name and address of the respondent

• whether the respondent is a child-minder or a provider of day care

• the address and type of accommodation where a child will, or may, be cared for.

3 The grounds for the application

The grounds are that a child is being looked after, or may be looked after

☐ by the registered child-minder who is named in paragraph 2

☐ under the provisions for day care made by the provider of that day care who is named in paragraph 2

and is suffering or is likely to suffer significant harm.

4 The order applied for

The Board or Trust applies to the court for an order for

☐ cancellation of the registration of the child-minder or provider of day care

☐ variation of a requirement imposed on the child-minder or provider of day care

☐ removal of a requirement, or imposing an additional requirement, on the child-minder or provider of day care.

5 The reason(s) for the application

If you are relying on a report or other documentary evidence, state the date(s) and author(s), and enclose a copy.

Signed (Applicant)   Date

29

FORM C7

SUPPLEMENT FOR AN APPLICATION FOR FINANCIAL PROVISION FOR A CHILD OR VARIATION OF FINANCIAL PROVISION FOR A CHILD

Schedule 1 Children (Northern Ireland) Order 1995

		[FAMILY PROCEEDINGS COURT]
of		
	Applicant	[PETTY SESSIONS DISTRICT]
of		
	Respondent	COUNTY COURT DIVISION OF

1 About the application

State whether you are seeking

- *an order for a lump sum; a transfer of property; a settlement of property; periodical payments; secured periodical payments*

or
- *a variation of an order for periodical payments; secured periodical payments; payment of a lump sum by instalments.*

2 Previous court orders and written agreements

If a written agreement or court order has been made a copy should be attached to this application.

If not available state
- *the date*
- *the terms*
- *the parties*
- *the court.*

3 The Child Support Agency

Assessment for maintenance

State whether the Agency has made an assessment   ☐ *Yes*   ☐ *No*
for the maintenance of the child(ren):

If Yes, state whether you are applying for additional child maintenance
- *because the Child Support Agency will no longer deal with your claim.*
  You should explain why the Agency will not deal with the claim.

or
- *on top of payments made through the Child Support Agency.*
  You should explain why you need additional maintenance and confirm that the Child Support Agency's assessment is the maximum amount obtainable.

Written agreement for maintenance

State whether there is a written maintenance   ☐ *Yes*   ☐ *No*
agreement:

If No, state whether you are applying for payment:

☐ for [a] stepchild[ren]

☐ in addition to child support maintenance already paid under a Child Support Agency assessment

30

☐ to meet expenses arising from the disability of [a] child[ren]

☐ to meet expenses incurred by [a] child[ren] in being educated or training for work

☐ when either the child[ren] OR the person with care of the child[ren] OR the absent parent of the child[ren] is not habitually resident in the United Kingdom

☐ for any other reason *(specify)*:

4 About the order

State the terms of the order you ask the court to make and in particular

● *the amount you would like the court to order*

● *whether you would like that amount paid weekly or monthly (if you are not applying for a lump sum)*

● *why you require the payments, or would like the court to carry an existing order.*

5 The collection of payment

If payments are not to be collected and paid to you by the Child Support Agency, give full details of how you would like payments collected. Possible ways are:

☐ **Directly to a bank, building society or post office account**

Give the full name and address, sorting code and the number of the account into which payment is to be made.

☐ **By an attachment of earnings order**

This is a court order which is sent to the employer of the person who is to pay.

☐ **If you would like the court to direct that money is paid in some other way**

Please say what method you would like.

And if you do not mind how the money is paid, please say so. The court will decide how it should be paid.

Signed	Date
(Applicant)	

You should now complete a Statement of Means, Form C7A

STATEMENT OF MEANS

Schedule 1 Children (Northern Ireland) Order 1995

of

Applicant

of

Respondent

[FAMILY PROCEEDINGS COURT AT]

[PETTY SESSIONS DISTRICT OF]

COUNTY COURT DIVISION OF

Warning The court will require to see written evidence of unemployment or sickness; or wage or salary slips, bank statements, and other papers giving details of your means. This evidence should be attached to this form or brought with you when you attend the hearing.

1 About you

State
- *your title, full name, address, telephone number and date of birth*
- *whether you are married, single or other*
- *whether you are the applicant or the respondent.*

2 Your dependants

State for each dependant
- *the dependant's title, full name and age*
- *whether the dependant is a spouse, partner, child or other*
- *whether the dependant is wholly or partially financially dependent on you*
- *whether the dependant lives with you.*

3 Your employment

State whether you are employed, self-employed or other.

If you are employed, state
- *your employment*
- *your employer's name, address and daytime telephone number.*

4 Your buildings and land

List all buildings and land you own, whether in your name alone or jointly, stating for each
- *the address*
- *the name(s) of the owner(s)*
- *the current value.*

5 Your financial assets

List each bank, building society and post office account, stating for each
- *the name and address where the account is held*
- *the account number*
- *the current balance*

*List all investments and securities (for example, shares, insurance policies)
stating for each one the name and quantity and current value.*

*List all pension schemes, stating for each one the scheme name and the
company.*

6 Other possessions of value

*List all possessions of value (for example, jewellery, antiques, collectable
items), stating for each:*

- *what they are*
- *the current value.*

7 Your income

<table>
<tr><td></td><td></td><td>State whether
Weekly (W) or
Monthly (M)</td></tr>
<tr><td>If employed, state your usual take home pay</td><td>£</td><td></td></tr>
<tr><td>If self-employed, state</td><td></td><td></td></tr>
<tr><td>• your drawings</td><td>£</td><td></td></tr>
<tr><td>• your gross turnover</td><td>£</td><td></td></tr>
<tr><td>• your profit after expenses</td><td>£</td><td></td></tr>
<tr><td>• whether you expect your turnover to increase,
decrease or remain the same:</td><td></td><td></td></tr>
<tr><td>• the date of the accounts showing the above
gross turnover and profit after expenses</td><td>Year ending 19</td><td></td></tr>
<tr><td>In all cases, state any of the following which you receive</td><td></td><td></td></tr>
<tr><td>• Income support</td><td>£</td><td></td></tr>
<tr><td>• Child Benefits</td><td>£</td><td></td></tr>
<tr><td>• Child Support Agency</td><td>£</td><td></td></tr>
<tr><td>• Other state benefits (specify source)</td><td>£
£
£</td><td></td></tr>
<tr><td>• Pension(s) (specify source)</td><td>£
£
£</td><td></td></tr>
<tr><td>• Contributions from others in the home (total)</td><td>£</td><td></td></tr>
<tr><td>• Other income (specify source and amount)</td><td>£
£
£
£</td><td></td></tr>
<tr><td>Total income:</td><td>£</td><td></td></tr>
</table>

8 Court Orders

Enclose a copy of any order

Court	Case Number	Amount outstanding (£)	Amount of payment (£)	Weekly (W) or Monthly (M)

9 Your expenses

	Amount of payments	Weekly (W) or Monthly (M)	Total debt	Amount of
Mortgage				
1st	_____	_____	_____	_____
2nd	_____	_____	_____	_____
Rent	_____	_____		_____
Rates	_____	_____		_____
Gas	_____	_____		_____
Electricity	_____	_____		_____
Telephone	_____	_____		_____
Water charges	_____	_____		_____
Credit Card	_____	_____	_____	_____
Loans	_____	_____	_____	_____
Storecards	_____	_____	_____	_____
HP Payments	_____	_____	_____	_____
TV rental and licence	_____	_____	_____	_____
Mail Order	_____	_____	_____	_____
Food	_____	_____		
Clothing	_____	_____		
Public transport	_____	_____		
Car expenses	_____	_____		
School meals	_____	_____		
Child minding	_____	_____		
Maintenance	_____	_____		
Child Support Agency	_____	_____		_____
Other payments (give details)	_____	_____		_____
	_____	_____	_____	_____
	_____	_____	_____	_____
Total Payments	_____	_____	_____	_____

Signed: [Applicant] [Respondent]	Date:

35

SUPPLEMENT FOR AN APPLICATION
FOR AN EMERGENCY PROTECTION ORDER

Article 63 Children (Northern Ireland) Order 1995

FAMILY PROCEEDINGS COURT AT

of

Applicant

of

Respondent

COUNTY COURT DIVISION OF

1 Description of the child(ren)

If a child's identity is not known, state details which will identify the child.

You may enclose a recent photograph of the child, which should be dated.

2 The grounds for the application

The grounds are

ANY APPLICANT	A ☐	that there is reasonable cause to believe that [this] [these] child[ren] [is] [are] likely to suffer significant harm if
		☐ the child[ren] [is] [are] not removed to accommodation by or on behalf of this applicant
	or	☐ the child[ren] [does] [do] not remain in the place where [the child] [they] [is] [are] currently being accommodated.
BOARD OR TRUST APPLICANTS	B ☐	that inquiries are being made about the welfare of the child[ren] under Article 66(1)(*b*) of the Children (Northern Ireland) Order 1995 **and** those enquiries are being frustrated by access to the child[ren] being unreasonably refused to someone who is authorised to seek access **and** there is reasonable cause to believe that access to the child[ren] is required as a matter of urgency.
AUTHORISED PERSON APPLICANTS	C ☐	that there is reasonable cause to suspect that the child[ren] [is] [are] suffering, or [is] [are] likely to suffer, significant harm **and** inquiries are being made with respect to the welfare of the child[ren] **and** those inquiries are being frustrated by access to the child[ren] being unreasonably refused to someone who is authorised to seek access **and** there is reasonable cause to believe that access to the child[ren] is required as a matter of urgency.

3 The additional order(s) applied for

☐ information on the whereabouts of the child[ren] (Article 67(1) of the Children (Northern Ireland) Order 1995).

☐ authorisation for entry of premises (Article 67(3) of the Children (Northern Ireland) Order 1995).

☐ authorisation to search for another child on the premises (Article 67(4) of the Children (Northern Ireland) Order 1995).

4 The direction(s) sought

☐ contact (Article 63(6)(*a*) of the Children (Northern Ireland) Order 1995).

☐ a medical or psychiatric examination or other assessment of the child[ren] (Article 63(6)(*b*) of the Children (Northern Ireland) Order 1995).

☐ to be accompanied by a registered medical practitioner, registered nurse or registered health visitor (Article 64(11) of the Children (Northern Ireland) Order 1995).

5 The reason(s) for the application

If you are relying on a report or other documentary evidence, state the date(s) and author(s) and enclose a copy.

| Signed (Applicant) | Date |

SUPPLEMENT FOR AN APPLICATION FOR A WARRANT TO ASSIST A PERSON AUTHORISED BY AN EMERGENCY PROTECTION ORDER

Article 67 Children (Northern Ireland) Order 1995

FAMILY PROCEEDINGS COURT AT

of

Applicant

of

Respondent

COUNTY COURT DIVISION OF

1 Description of the child[ren]

If a child's identity is not known, state details which will identify the child.
You may enclose a recent photograph of the child, which should be dated.

2 The grounds for the application

An emergency protection order was made on:
(State the date and time, and attach a copy of the order)

and ☐ a person **has been** prevented from exercising powers under the order by being refused entry to premises or access to the child[ren]

or

☐ that a person **is likely to be** prevented from exercising powers under the order by being refused entry to premises or access to the child[ren].

3 The direction(s) sought

State
- *whether you wish to accompany the constable, if the warrant is granted*
- *whether you wish the constable to be accompanied by a registered medical practitioner, registered nurse or registered health visitor, if he so wishes*
- *where the constable is to take the child, if the warrant is executed.*

4 The reason(s) for the application

If you are relying on a report or other documentary evidence, state the date(s) and author(s) and enclose a copy.

Signed   Date
(Applicant)

FORM C10

SUPPLEMENT FOR AN APPLICATION FOR A CARE OR SUPERVISION ORDER

Article 50 Children (Northern Ireland) Order 1995

FAMILY PROCEEDINGS COURT AT

of

Applicant

of

Respondent

COUNTY COURT DIVISION OF

---

1 The grounds for the application

The grounds are that the child[ren] [is] [are] suffering or [is] [are] likely to suffer, significant harm and the harm, or likelihood of harm, is attributable to

☐ the care given to the child[ren], or likely to be given to the child[ren] if the order were not made, not being what it would be reasonable to expect a parent to give to the child[ren]

☐ the child[ren] being beyond parental control.

2 The reason(s) for the application

If you are relying on a report or other documentary evidence, state the date(s) and author(s) and enclose a copy.

3 Your plans for the child(ren)

Include • *in the case of supervision orders only, any requirements which you will invite the court to impose pursuant to paragraph 3 Schedule 3 Children (Northern Ireland) Order 1995*

• *in all cases, whether you will invite the court to make an interim order.*

4 The direction(s) sought

Signed
(Applicant)

Date

FORM C11

SUPPLEMENT FOR AN APPLICATION FOR
AUTHORITY TO REFUSE CONTACT WITH A CHILD IN CARE

Article 53(4) Children (Northern Ireland) Order 1995

FAMILY PROCEEDINGS COURT AT

of

    Applicant

of

    Respondent

COUNTY COURT DIVISION OF

---

1 The current arrangements for contact

State   • *the full name(s) of the child(ren)*

       • *the full name(s) of each person who has contact with each child and the current arrangements for contact*

       • *whether the Board or Trust has refused contact for 7 days or less.*

2 The order applied for

State the full name and relationship of any person in respect of whom authority to refuse contact with each child is sought.

3 The reason(s) for the application

If you are relying on a report or other documentary evidence state the date(s) and author(s) and enclose a copy.

Signed   Date
(Applicant)

FORM C12

SUPPLEMENT FOR AN APPLICATION FOR CONTACT WITH A CHILD IN CARE

Article 53(2) and (3) Children (Northern Ireland) Order 1995

FAMILY PROCEEDINGS COURT AT

of

Applicant

of

Respondent

COUNTY COURT DIVISION OF

1 State the full name(s) of the child(ren)

2 Your relationship to the child(ren)

State whether

- *you are a parent or guardian*
- *you hold a residence order which was in force immediately before the care order was made*
- *you had care of the child(ren) through an order which was in force immediately before the care order was made.*

3 The order applied for and your reason(s) for the application

If you are relying on a report or other documentary evidence, state the date(s) and author(s) and enclose a copy.

Signed   Date
(Applicant)

41

SUPPLEMENT FOR AN APPLICATION FOR
A CHILD ASSESSMENT ORDER

Article 62 Children (Northern Ireland) Order 1995

FAMILY PROCEEDINGS COURT AT

of

     Applicant

of

     Respondent

COUNTY COURT DIVISION OF

1 The grounds for the application

The grounds are   that there is reasonable cause to suspect that the child[ren] [is] [are] suffering, or [is] [are] likely to suffer, significant harm

and

an assessment of the state of the child[ren]'s health or development or of the way in which the child[ren] [has] [have] been treated, is required to determine whether or not the child[ren] [is] [are] suffering, or [is] [are] likely to suffer, significant harm

and

it is unlikely that such an assessment will be made, or be satisfactory, in the absence of an order under this section.

State your reason(s) for believing the grounds exist.

If you are relying on a report or other documentary evidence, state the date(s) and author(s) and enclose a copy.

2 The direction(s) sought in respect of the assessment

3 The direction(s) sought in respect of contact

Signed	Date
(Applicant)	

FORM C14

SUPPLEMENT FOR AN APPLICATION FOR
AN EDUCATION SUPERVISION ORDER

Article 55 Children (Northern Ireland) Order 1995

Paragraph 6 Schedule 4 Children (Northern Ireland) Order 1995

FAMILY PROCEEDINGS COURT AT

of

    Applicant

of

    Respondent

COUNTY COURT DIVISION OF

1 Prior consultation

State the name of the Board or Trust which has been consulted:

☐ The Board or Trust is the authority providing the child[ren] with accommodation or on whose behalf the child[ren] [is] [are] being provided with accommodation.

or

☐ the Board or Trust is the authority within whose area the child[ren] live[s], or will live.

2 The grounds for the application

The ground is that the child[ren] [is] [are] of compulsory school age and [is] [are] not being properly educated.

State your reason(s) for believing the ground exists. If you are relying on a report or other documentary evidence, state the date(s) and author(s) and enclose a copy.

3 The order and direction(s) applied for

Signed   Date

(Applicant)

SUPPLEMENT FOR AN APPLICATION FOR
AN EXTENSION OF AN EDUCATION SUPERVISION ORDER

Paragraph 5(2) of Schedule 4 to the Children (Northern Ireland) Order 1995

FAMILY PROCEEDINGS COURT AT

of

Applicant

of

Respondent

COUNTY COURT DIVISION OF

1 About the Education Supervision Order
State when the order was made and when it is due to end.
Enclose a copy of the order.

2 The extension
State your reason(s) for asking the court to extend the order. If you are relying on a report or other documentary evidence, state the date(s) and author(s) and enclose a copy.

Signed   Date
(Applicant)

SUPPLEMENT FOR AN APPLICATION FOR
A RECOVERY ORDER

Article 69 Children (Northern Ireland) Order 1995

FAMILY PROCEEDINGS COURT AT

of

    Applicant

of

    Respondent

COUNTY COURT DIVISION OF

1 Particulars of the child(ren)

State whether the child[ren] [is] [are]   ☐ in care

or ☐ the subject of an emergency protection order

or ☐ in police protection

Enclose a copy of the order

If a child's identity is not known, state details that will identify the child.
You may enclose a recent photograph of the child, which should be dated.

2 The order and direction(s) applied for

State • *whether the child(ren) (is) (are) to be produced to an authorised person specified by the court (Article 69(7) Children (Northern Ireland) Order 1995)*

• *whether you require the court to authorise a constable to enter specified premises (Article 69(3)(d) Children (Northern Ireland) Order 1995).*

3 The grounds for the application

The grounds are that the child[ren] ☐ [has] [have] been unlawfully taken away or [is] [are] being unlawfully kept away from the responsible person

or ☐ [has] [have] run away or [is] [are] staying away from the responsible person

or ☐ [is] [are] missing.

4 The reason(s) for the application

Include your ground(s) for believing that the child(ren) (is) (are) on the premises named in paragraph 2 above (if applicable) (Article 69(6) Children (Northern Ireland) Order 1995).

If your are relying on a report or other documentary evidence, state the date(s) and author(s) and enclose a copy.

Signed
(Applicant)

Date

APPLICATION FOR A WARRANT OF ASSISTANCE

Article 178 Children (Northern Ireland) Order 1995

FAMILY PROCEEDINGS COURT AT

of

Applicant

of

Respondent

COUNTY COURT DIVISION OF

---

1 State the full name(s) of the child(ren) (if known)

2 About you (the applicant)

State
- your title, full name, address, telephone number, and relationship to the child(ren) (if any)
- your solicitor's name, address, reference, telephone, FAX and DX numbers
- whether you are:
  - ☐ a person authorised by a Board or Trust
  - ☐ a person authorised by the Department
  - ☐ a supervisor acting under a supervision order

3 Description of the child(ren) (if applicable)

If a child's identity is not known, state details which will identify the child. You may enclose a recent photograph of the child, which should be dated.

4 The grounds for the application

☐ I am attempting to exercise powers under an enactment within Article 178 of the Children (Northern Ireland) Order 1995 at the following premises (*give full address*):

and

☐ **I have been** prevented from exercising those powers by

☐ **I am likely to be** prevented from exercising those powers by

PERSON
AUTHORISED
BY THE
AUTHORITY

Article 77(5)
- [being, or likely to be, refused entry to accommodation provided by a voluntary organisation]
- [being, or likely to be, refused access to a child in accommodation provided by a voluntary organisation]

Article 93
- [being, or likely to be, refused entry to a children's home]
- [being, or likely to be, refused access to a child in a children's home]
- [being, or likely to be, refused access to records kept in a children's home]

Article 108
- [being, or likely to be, refused entry to a private foster home]
- [being, or likely to be, refused access to a child in a private foster home]

Article 130
- [being, or likely to be, refused entry to domestic premises where child-minding is carried on]
- [being, or likely to be, refused access to a child on domestic premises where child-minding is carried on]
- [being, or likely to be, refused access to records kept in domestic premises where child-minding is carried on]
- [being, or likely to be, refused entry to premises on which day care for children under the age of 12 is provided]
- [being, or likely to be, refused access to a child in premises on which day care for children under the age of 12 is provided]
- [being, or likely to be, refused access to records kept on premises on which day care for children under the age of 12 is provided]

Article 175
- [being, or likely to be, refused entry to a residential care, nursing or mental nursing home]
- [being, or likely to be, refused access to a child in a residential care, nursing or mental nursing home]

Article 176
- [being, or likely to be, refused entry to an independent school]
- [being, or likely to be, refused access to a child in an independent school]

Article 34 Adoption (Northern Ireland) Order 1987
- [being, or likely to be, refused entry to premises on which a protected child is, or is likely to be, kept]
- [being, or likely to be, prevented from visiting a protected child]

PERSON AUTHORISED BY THE DEPARTMENT	*Article 149*	[being, or likely to be, refused entry to any of the premises specified by Article 149] ☐ [being, or likely to be, refused access to a child in any of the premises specified by Article 149] [being, or likely to be, refused access to records stored in any of the premises specified in Article 149]
SUPERVISOR UNDER THE SUPERVISION ORDER	*Paragraph 7(1)(b) Schedule 3*	☐ [being, or likely to be, refused entry to accommodation where a supervised child is living]
	Paragraph 7(2)(b) Schedule 3	☐ [being, or likely to be, refused contact with a supervised child by a responsible person]

4 The respondent(s)

For each respondent state the title, full name, address, telephone number and relationship (if any) to each child.

5 The reason(s) for the application

If you are relying on a report or other documentary evidence, state the date(s) and author(s) and enclose a copy.

6 The direction(s) sought

State ● *whether you wish to accompany the constable, if the warrant is granted*

● *whether you wish the constable to be accompanied by a registered medical practitioner, registered nurse or registered health visitor, if he so wishes.*

Signed   Date
(Applicant)

SUPPLEMENT FOR AN APPLICATION FOR AN ORDER
TO HOLD A CHILD IN SECURE ACCOMMODATION

Article 44 Children (Northern Ireland) Order 1995

FAMILY PROCEEDINGS COURT AT

of

Applicant

of

Respondent

COUNTY COURT DIVISION OF

1 The grounds for the application

The grounds are ☐ that the child[ren] [has] [have] a history of absconding and [is] [are] likely to abscond from any other accommodation and if the child[ren] abscond [he] [she] [they] [is] [are] likely to suffer significant harm.

☐ that if the child[ren] [is] [are] kept in any other accommodation, [the child] [they] [is] [are] likely to injure [himself] [herself] [themselves] or other people.

(In the case of a child under the age of 13) ☐ the approval of the Department of Health and Social Services to the placement of the child[ren] in secure accommodation has been granted and is attached.

2 The reason(s) for the application and length of order applied for

If you are relying on a report or other documentary evidence, state the date(s) and author(s) and enclose a copy.

Signed
(Applicant)

Date

FORM C18

ORDER OR DIRECTION

Children (Northern Ireland) Order 1995

	[FAMILY PROCEEDINGS COURT AT]
Applicant	
of	[PETTY SESSIONS DISTRICT OF]
Respondent	
of	[COUNTY COURT DIVISION OF]

The full name(s) of the child(ren) Date(s) of birth Child(ren)'s number(s)

[Order]   [Direction]

Signed

CHILDREN (NORTHERN IRELAND) ORDER 1995

Record of the Hearing

Applicant

Respondent

The full name(s) of the child(ren)

On notice ☐   Ex parte ☐

Attendees

Name   Present   Represented by

Evidence

The court read the report(s)/statement(s) of   Dated

*To be
completed
only when
the court
makes a
finding
of fact*

The court heard oral evidence [on oath] of

CHILDREN (NORTHERN IRELAND) ORDER 1995

FAMILY PROCEEDINGS COURT AT

Applicant

Respondent

COUNTY COURT DIVISION OF

Order   Emergency Protection Order

Article 63 Children (Northern Ireland) Order 1995

The full name(s) of the child(ren) Boy or Girl Date(s) of birth

[described as]

Warning   **It is an offence intentionally to obstruct any person exercising the power under Article 63(4)(b) Children (Northern Ireland) Order 1995 to remove, or prevent the removal, of a child (Article 63(15) Children (Northern Ireland) Order 1995)**

The court grants   an Emergency Protection Order to the applicant who is

The order gives the applicant parental responsibility for the child[ren].

The court authorises   [the applicant to remove the child[ren] to accommodation provided by or on behalf of the applicant]

[the applicant to prevent the child[ren] being removed from].

[This order directs that   any person who can produce the child[ren] to the applicant must do so.]

The court directs that

This order has [not] been made ex parte

This order ends on   at   [am]   [pm]

Ordered by

on   at   [am]   [pm]

Notes about the Emergency Protection Order

About this order	This is an Emergency Protection Order.

About this order

This is an Emergency Protection Order.

This order states what has been authorised in respect of the child[ren] and when the order will end.

The court can extend this order for up to 7 days but it can only do this once.

Warning

If you are shown this order, you must comply with it. If you do not, you may commit an offence. Read the order now.

What you may do

you may apply to the court

to **change the directions**

or to **end the order.**

You may apply at any time, but the court will only hear an application to end an order **when 72 hours** have passed since the order was made.

If you would like to ask the court to change the directions, or end the order, you must fill in a form. You can obtain the form from a court office.

If the court has directed that the child[ren] should have a medical, psychiatric or another kind of examination, you may ask the court to allow a doctor of your choice to be at the examination.

What you should do

Go to a solicitor as soon as you can.

Some solicitors specialise in court proceedings which involve children. You can obtain the address of a solicitor or an advice agency from the Yellow Pages or the Law Society.

A solicitor or an advice agency will be able to tell you whether you may be eligible for legal aid.

FORM C21

CHILDREN (NORTHERN IRELAND) ORDER 1995

FAMILY PROCEEDINGS COURT AT

of

Applicant

of

Respondent

COUNTY COURT DIVISION OF

Order [Variation of an Emergency Protection Order direction
(Article 63(9)(*b*) Children (Northern Ireland) Order 1995)]
[Extension of an Emergency Protection Order
(Article 64(4) Children (Northern Ireland) Order 1995)]
[Discharge of an Emergency Protection Order
(Article 64(7) Children (Northern Ireland) Order 1995)]

The full name(s) of the child(ren)   Date(s) of birth

The court [extends]
[varies] [discharges]   [the direction[s] given] [the Emergency Protection Order
granted] by [this court] the

court]

on   at   [am]   [pm]

[The direction(s) are
[varied as follows]

[The order now ends on]

Ordered by

on   at   [am]   [pm]

FORM C22

CHILDREN (NORTHERN IRELAND) ORDER 1995

FAMILY PROCEEDINGS COURT AT

of

Applicant

of

Respondent

COUNTY COURT DIVISION OF

Warrant   To assist a person authorised by an Emergency Protection Order
           Article 67(9) Children (Northern Ireland) Order 1995

To all Police Constables

The court was satisfied that

who is the applicant, has been prevented, or is likely to be prevented from exercising powers under an Emergency Protection Order by being refused entry to the named premises or access to the child concerned.

The court authorises

you to assist the applicant to exercise powers under an Emergency Protection Order made on

You may use reasonable force if necessary.

You may assist the applicant
to gain access **to the child**   *Name*

Boy or Girl   *Date of birth*

described as

You may assist the applicant
to gain entry **to the
premises**   *known as*

The court directs

[that you should not be accompanied by the person who applied for the warrant]

[that you may, if you wish, be accompanied by

     a registered medical practitioner

or   a registered nurse

or   a registered health visitor]

You should execute this warrant in accordance with the orders and directions contained in the Emergency Protection Order.

This warrant has	[not] been made ex parte.		
This warrant ends on			
Ordered by			
on	at	[am]	[pm]

CHILDREN (NORTHERN IRELAND) ORDER 1995

FAMILY PROCEEDINGS COURT AT

of

Applicant

of

Respondent

COUNTY COURT DIVISION OF

Order   Authority to keep a child in Secure Accommodation
             Article 44 Children (Northern Ireland) Order 1995

The full name(s) of the child   Date of birth

The court authorises

to keep the child in secure accommodation until

This order has been
made on the ground
that   [the child has a history of absconding and is likely to
              abscond from any other accommodation, and if the child
              absconds [he] [she] is likely to suffer significant harm]

              [if the child is kept in any other accommodation the child
              is likely to injure [himself] [herself] or other persons]

[The court was satisfied   that the child, not being legally represented, had been
              informed of [his] [her] right to apply for legal aid and
              having had the opportunity to apply, had refused or failed
              to apply]

Ordered by

on

CHILDREN (NORTHERN IRELAND) ORDER 1995

FAMILY PROCEEDINGS COURT AT

of

Applicant

of

Respondent

COUNTY COURT DIVISION OF

Order	Authority to search for another child
	Article 67(4) Children (Northern Ireland) Order 1995

The full name(s) of the child	Boy or Girl	Date of birth

[who is described as]

The court was satisfied that

[an order has been granted on
to the applicant for the emergency protection of a
child, *known as*

and that the order had authorised the applicant to
enter these premises].
[there was reasonable cause to believe that the child
named in this order may be on those premises and
that an Emergency Protection Order ought to be
made in respect of that child].

The court authorises

who is the applicant

to enter the premises, *known as*

and search for the child.

Warning
**It is an offence intentionally to obstruct the
applicant from entering or searching the
premises specified above (Article 67(4) and (7)
Children (Northern Ireland) Order 1995).**

This order has [not] been made ex parte.

This order ends on

59

Ordered by

Signed

on   at   [am]   [pm]

CHILDREN (NORTHERN IRELAND) ORDER 1995

FAMILY PROCEEDINGS COURT AT

of

      Applicant

of

      Respondent

COUNTY COURT DIVISION OF

Warrant   To assist a person to gain access to a child or entry to premises
        Article 178 Children (Northern Ireland) Order 1995

To all Police Constables

The court authorises   you to assist

exercise powers under an enactment as specified on the reverse of this warrant.

You may use reasonable force if necessary.

[You may assist this person to gain access **to the child**]   *Name*

Boy or Girl   *Date of birth*

described as

[You may assist this person to gain entry **to the premises**]

known as

The court directs   [that you should not be accompanied by the person who applied for the warrant]

[that you may, if you wish, be accompanied by
      a registered medical practitioner
or   a registered nurse
or   a registered health visitor]

This warrant has   [not] been made ex parte.

Ordered by   Signed

on   at   [am]   [pm]

The court is satisfied that the applicant
- ☐ has been prevented from exercising those powers by
- ☐ is likely to be prevented from exercising those powers by

PERSON AUTHORISED BY THE LOCAL AUTHORITY

Article 77(5) ☐
[being, or likely to be, refused entry to accommodation provided by a voluntary organisation]
[being, or likely to be, refused access to a child in accommodation provided by a voluntary organisation]

Article 93 ☐
[being, or likely to be, refused entry to a children's home]
[being, or likely to be, refused access to a child in a children's home]

Article 108 ☐
[being, or likely to be, refused entry to a private foster home]
[being, or likely to be, refused access to a child in a private foster home]

Article 130 ☐
[being, or likely to be, refused entry to domestic premises where child-minding is carried on]
[being, or likely to be, refused access to a child on domestic premises where child-minding is carried on]
[being, or likely to be, refused access to records kept on domestic premises where child-minding is carried on]
[being, or likely to be, refused access to a child in premises on which day care for children under the age of 12 is provided] ☐

Article 175 ☐
[being, or likely to be, refused entry to a residential care, nursing or mental nursing home]
[being, or likely to be, refused entry to premises on which day care for children under the age of 12 is carried out]
[being, or likely to be, refused access to a child in a residential care, nursing or mental nursing home]
[being, or likely to be, refused access to records kept on premises on which day care for children under the age of 12 is provided]

Article 176 ☐
[being, or likely to be, refused entry to an independent school]
[being, or likely to be, refused access to a child in an independent school]

PERSON AUTHORISED BY THE DEPARTMENT	*Article 149*	☐ [being, or likely to be, refused entry to any of the premises specified by Article 149] [being, or likely to be, refused access to a child in any of the premises specified by Article 149]
	Article 34 Adoption (Northern Ireland) Order 1987	☐ [being, or likely to be, refused entry to premises on which a protected child is, or is likely to be, kept] [being, or likely to be, refused access to a protected child]
SUPERVISOR UNDER THE SUPERVISION ORDER	*Paragraph 7(1)(b) Schedule 3*	☐ [being, or likely to be, refused entry to accommodation where a supervised child is living]
	Paragraph 7(2)(b) Schedule 3	☐ [being, or likely to be, refused contact with a supervised child by a responsible person]

CHILDREN (NORTHERN IRELAND) ORDER 1995

FAMILY PROCEEDINGS COURT AT

of

Applicant

of

Respondent

COUNTY COURT DIVISION OF

Order	Recovery of a child Article 69 Children (Northern Ireland) Order 1995

The full name(s) of the child	Boy or Girl	Date of birth

| The court is satisfied that | [has parental responsibility for the child by virtue of a [Care Order] [Emergency Protection Order] made on   ]
[the child is in police protection and the designated officer is   ] |
|---|---|

[The court authorises	[a police constable] to remove the child.]
Warning	**It is an offence intentionally to obstruct the person from removing the child (Article 69(9) Children (Northern Ireland) Order 1995)**
[The court authorises	[a police constable to enter the premises, *known as* and search for the child, using reasonable force if necessary.]
[The court requires	any person who has information about where the child is, or may be, to give that information to a police constable **or** an officer of the court, if asked to do so.]
[The court directs	any person who can produce the child when asked to by
[a police constable] to do so.]

This order has	[not] been made ex parte.
Ordered by	
on	

CHILDREN (NORTHERN IRELAND) ORDER 1995

FAMILY PROCEEDINGS COURT AT

of

Applicant

of

Respondent

COUNTY COURT DIVISION OF

Order	[Care Order
	Article 50 Children (Northern Ireland) Order 1995]
	[Discharge of a Care Order
	Article 58(1) Children (Northern Ireland) Order 1995]

The full name(s) of the child[ren]   Date(s) of birth

[The court orders   [that the child[ren] be placed in the care of
                                                        Board/Trust]

[The court discharges   [the Care Order made by [this court] [the
                                                                court]
                            on   ]

Warning

While a Care Order is in force no person may cause the child[ren] to be known by a new surname or remove the child[ren] from the United Kingdom without the written consent of every person with parental responsibility for the child[ren] or the leave of the court.

However, the authority, in whose care [a] [the] child[ren] [is] [are], may remove that child from the United Kingdom for a period of less than 1 month.

It may be a criminal offence under the Child Abduction (Northern Ireland) Order 1985 to remove the child[ren] from the United Kingdom without the leave of the court.

Ordered by

on

CHILDREN (NORTHERN IRELAND) ORDER 1995

FAMILY PROCEEDINGS COURT AT

of

Applicant

of

Respondent

COUNTY COURT DIVISION OF

| Order | Interim Care Order |
| | Article 57 Children (Northern Ireland) Order 1995 |

The full name(s) of the child[ren]   Date(s) of birth

The court orders   that the child[ren] be placed in the care of
                                                                Board/Trust

The order expires on

[The court directs]

Warning

While a Care Order is in force no person may cause the child[ren] to be known by a new surname or remove the child[ren] from the United Kingdom without the written consent of every person with parental responsibility for the child[ren] or the leave of the court.

However, the authority, in whose care a child is, may remove that child from the United Kingdom for a period of less than 1 month.

It may be a criminal offence under the Child Abduction (Northern Ireland) Order 1985 to remove the child[ren] from the United Kingdom without the leave of the court.

Ordered by

on

CHILDREN (NORTHERN IRELAND) ORDER 1995

FAMILY PROCEEDINGS COURT AT

of

Applicant

of

Respondent

COUNTY COURT DIVISION OF

Order [Contact with a child in care
Article 53(2) and (3) Children (Northern Ireland) Order 1995]
[Authority to refuse contact with a child in care
Article 53(4) Children (Northern Ireland) Order 1995]

The full name(s) of the child[ren]   Date(s) of birth

The authority

The court orders that   [there may be contact between the child[ren] and]

[the authority is authorised to refuse contact between the child[ren] and]

[The contact is subject
to the following
conditions]

[Notice   Any authority may refuse to allow the contact that would otherwise
be required by virtue of Article 53(1) of the Children (Northern
Ireland) Order 1995 or an order under this section if (a) they are
satisfied that it is necessary to do so in order to safeguard or
promote the welfare of the child[ren]; and (b) the refusal (i) is
decided upon as a matter of urgency; and (ii) does not last for more
than 7 days (Article 53(6) Children (Northern Ireland) Order
1995).]

Ordered by

on

CHILDREN (NORTHERN IRELAND) ORDER 1995

FAMILY PROCEEDINGS COURT AT

of

Applicant

of

Respondent

COUNTY COURT DIVISION OF

Order   [Supervision Order]
Article 50 and Schedule 3 Children (Northern Ireland) Order 1995
[Interim Supervision Order]
Article 57 and Schedule 3 Children (Northern Ireland) Order 1995

The full name(s) of the child[ren]   Date(s) of birth

The court orders

to supervise the child[ren]   [for a period of   months from the date of this order]
[for the interim period of   ]

The court directs

Ordered by

on

FORM C31

CHILDREN (NORTHERN IRELAND) ORDER 1995

FAMILY PROCEEDINGS COURT AT

of

Applicant

of

Respondent

COUNTY COURT DIVISION OF

Order

[Substitution of a Supervision Order for a Care Order
Article 58(4) Children (Northern Ireland) Order 1995]
[Discharge] [Variation] of a Supervision Order
Article 58(2) and (3) of the Children (Northern Ireland) Order 1995
[Extension of a Supervision Order
Paragraph 6(3) Schedule 3 Children (Northern Ireland) Order 1995]

The full name(s) of the child[ren]   Date(s) of birth

The court [substitutes]
[discharges] [varies]
[extends]   the [Supervision Order] [for the] [Care Order]

made by   [this court] [the

court]

on

The court orders

to supervise the child[ren].

The court directs

[This order ends on   ]

Ordered by

on

CHILDREN (NORTHERN IRELAND) ORDER 1995

[FAMILY PROCEEDINGS COURT AT]

of

Applicant   [PETTY SESSIONS DISTRICT OF]

of

Respondent

COUNTY COURT DIVISION OF

Order	Education Supervision Order
	Article 55 Children (Northern Ireland) Order 1995

The full name(s) of the child[ren]   Date(s) of birth

Warning   **A parent of the child[ren] may be guilty of an offence if he or she persistently fails to comply with a direction given by the supervisor under this order while it is in force**

(Paragraph 8 Schedule 4 Children (Northern Ireland) Order 1995)

The court was satisfied   that the child[ren] [was] [were] of compulsory school age and [was] [were] not being properly educated.

The court orders

education and library board

to supervise the child[ren]   [for a period of 12 months beginning on the date of this order]

[until the child[ren] [is] [are] no longer of compulsory school age].

Ordered by

on

CHILDREN (NORTHERN IRELAND) ORDER 1995

of

Applicant

[FAMILY PROCEEDINGS COURT AT]

[PETTY SESSIONS DISTRICT OF]

of

Respondent

COUNTY COURT DIVISION OF

Order
[Discharge of an Education Supervision Order
Paragraph 7 Schedule 4 Children (Northern Ireland) Order 1995]
[Extension of an Education Supervision Order
Paragraph 5 Schedule 4 Children (Northern Ireland) Order 1995]

The full name(s) of the child[ren]   Date(s) of birth

The court
[discharges]
[extends]   the Education Supervision Order

made by   [this court] [the

court]

on

requiring

education and library board to supervise the child[ren].

[The court directs
under Paragraph 7(2) Schedule 4 Children (Northern Ireland) Order 1995

Board [Trust] shall investigate the circumstances of the child[ren]]

[This order ends on   ]

Ordered by

on

FORM C34

CHILDREN (NORTHERN IRELAND) ORDER 1995

FAMILY PROCEEDINGS COURT AT

of

Applicant

of

Respondent

COUNTY COURT DIVISION OF

Order   Child Assessment Order
Article 62 Children (Northern Ireland) Order 1995

The full name(s) of the child   Date of birth

The court orders   a [medical] [psychiatric] [
                            ] assessment of the child.

The court directs that
[the child is to be
assessed at

[the child is to be
assessed by

[the child may be kept
away from home and
stay at   from

        to

        While away from home, the child must be allowed contact
with

the assessment is to
begin by

        and last no more than   days from the date it begins.

Notice   Any person who is in a position to produce the child must
do so to

        and must comply with the directions in this order.

Ordered by

on

CHILDREN (NORTHERN IRELAND) ORDER 1995

| | [FAMILY PROCEEDINGS COURT AT] |
| of | [PETTY SESSIONS DISTRICT OF] |

Applicant

of

Respondent

COUNTY COURT DIVISION OF

| Direction | To undertake an investigation |
| | Article 56 Children (Northern Ireland) Order 1995 |

| The full name(s) of the child[ren] | Date(s) of birth |

| It appears to the court | that it may be appropriate for a Care or Supervision Order to be made in respect of the child[ren]. |

The court directs	the
	Board/Trust
	to investigate the circumstances of the child[ren].

| [The court directs | copies of the following documents |
| | shall be served on the Board/Trust.] |

| **Reporting the result** | The Board/Trust must report to the court [the Family Proceedings Court], in writing, under Article 56 of the Children (Northern Ireland) Order 1995 |

Ordered by

on

FORM C35A

EDUCATION AND LIBRARIES (NORTHERN IRELAND) ORDER 1986:
Schedule 13 paragraph 6

PETTY SESSIONS DISTRICT OF

COUNTY COURT DIVISION OF

Following the prosecution of   under paragraph 4 of
Schedule 13 to the Education and Libraries (Northern Ireland) Order 1986.

The court directs   education and libraries board
to apply for an education supervision order under the Children (Northern Ireland)
Order 1995. [The application is to be made to the Family Proceedings Court at
]

Ordered by

FORM C36

CHILDREN (NORTHERN IRELAND) ORDER 1995

[FAMILY PROCEEDINGS COURT AT]

of

Applicant   [PETTY SESSIONS DISTRICT OF]

of

Respondent

COUNTY COURT DIVISION OF

Order   Family Assistance Order
Article 16 Children (Northern Ireland) Order 1995

The full name(s) of the child[ren]   Date(s) of birth

The court orders   [an officer of

Board/Trust]
to be made available to advise, assist and, where appropriate, befriend

[The court directs]

This order ends on

Notice   This Order will have effect for 6 months from the date below, or such lesser period as specified.

Ordered by

on

FORM C37

CHILDREN (NORTHERN IRELAND) ORDER 1995

		[FAMILY PROCEEDINGS COURT AT]
of		
	Applicant	[PETTY SESSIONS DISTRICT OF]
of		
	Respondent	
		COUNTY COURT DIVISION OF

Order	[Residence] [Contact] [Specific Issue] [Prohibited Steps] Order Article 8 Children (Northern Ireland) Order 1995	
	The full name(s) of the child[ren]	Date(s) of birth

The court orders

Warning	Where a Residence Order is in force no person may cause the child[ren] to be known by a new surname or remove the child[ren] from the United Kingdom without the written consent of every person with parental responsibility for the child[ren] or the leave of the court.
	However, this does not prevent the removal of [a] child[ren], for a period of less than 1 month, by the person in whose favour the Residence Order is made (Article 13(1) and (2) Children (Northern Ireland) Order 1995).
	It may be a criminal offence under the Child Abduction (Northern Ireland) Order 1985 to remove the child[ren] from the United Kingdom without the leave of the court.
Notice	Any person with parental responsibility for [a] child[ren] may obtain advice on what can be done to prevent the issue of a passport to the child[ren]. They should write to The United Kingdom Passport Agency, Clive House, Petty France, LONDON, SW1H 9HD.
Ordered by	
on	

CHILDREN (NORTHERN IRELAND) ORDER 1995

FAMILY PROCEEDINGS COURT AT

of

Applicant

of

Respondent

COUNTY COURT DIVISION OF

Order   [Leave to change the surname by which a child is known
            Article 13(1) 52(7) Children (Northern Ireland) Order 1995]
            [Leave to remove a child from the United Kingdom
            Article 13(1) 52(7) Children (Northern Ireland) Order 1995]

The full name(s) of the child[ren]   Date(s) of birth

The court grants leave to

[to change the child[ren]'s
surname to

[and] [to remove the   from the United Kingdom
child[ren]]
                            [permanently] [until]

Ordered by

        on

CHILDREN (NORTHERN IRELAND) ORDER 1995

[FAMILY PROCEEDINGS COURT AT]

of

Applicant   [PETTY SESSIONS DISTRICT OF]

of

Respondent

COUNTY COURT DIVISION OF

Order	[Parental Responsibility Order Article 7(1) Children (Northern Ireland) Order 1995] [Termination of a Parental Responsibility Order Article 7(3) Children (Northern Ireland) Order 1995]

The full name(s) of the child[ren]   Date(s) of birth

The court orders that

shall [no longer] have parental responsibility for the child[ren].

Notice	A parental responsibility order can only end
	(a) When the child reaches 18 years
	(b) By order of the court made
	   ● on the application of any person who has parental responsibility
	   ● with leave of the court on application of the child.

Ordered by

on

FORM C40

CHILDREN (NORTHERN IRELAND) ORDER 1995

FAMILY PROCEEDINGS COURT AT

of

Applicant

of

Respondent

COUNTY COURT DIVISION OF

Order	[Cancellation of the registration of a child-minder or a provider of day care]
	[Removal, Variation or Imposition of a requirement on a child-minder or a provider of day care]
	Article 129 Children (Northern Ireland) Order 1995

[The court [cancels] the registration of

who is a [child-minder] [provider of day care] and who is looking after, or may look after, a child.]

[The court [removes]
[varies] [imposes]]   a requirement on

who is a [child-minder] [provider of day care] and who is looking after, or may look after, a child.

The requirement
[removed] [varied]
[imposed]   [was] [is]

This order has   [not] been made ex parte.

Ordered by

on

79

CHILDREN (NORTHERN IRELAND) ORDER 1995

FAMILY PROCEEDINGS COURT AT

of

Applicant

of

Respondent

COUNTY COURT DIVISION OF

Order   [Making or refusing the appointment of a guardian ad litem
Article 60 Children (Northern Ireland) Order 1995]
[Termination of the appointment of a guardian ad litem]

The full name(s) of the child[ren]   Date(s) of birth

The court   [appoints] [refuses to appoint] [terminate the appointment of] [a[s] guardian ad litem] for the child[ren] in the proceedings

☐ for a Care Order or Supervision Order
☐ for discharge of a Care Order
☐ for variation or discharge of a Supervision Order
☐ for substitution of a Supervision Order for a Care Order
☐ for Contact, or Refusal of Contact, with a child in care
☐ for consideration of a Residence Order for a child in care
☐ under Article 33 Children (Northern Ireland) Order 1995
☐ under Paragraph 6(3) Schedule 3 Children (Northern Ireland) Order 1995
☐ under Part VI Children (Northern Ireland) Order 1995 (specify)
☐ where a Direction under Article 56(1) Children (Northern Ireland) Order 1995 has been made and the court [has made] [is considering] whether to make an [Interim Care Order] [Supervision Order]
☐ under Article 52(7) Children (Northern Ireland) Order 1995
☐ under Article 52(7) Children (Northern Ireland) Order 1995
☐ under Article 44 Children (Northern Ireland) Order 1995
☐ concerning an Appeal against a determination in any of the above proceedings
☐ other proceedings which are

The appointment shall continue until [   ]
[terminated by the court]

Ordered by

on

CHILDREN (NORTHERN IRELAND) ORDER 1995

FAMILY PROCEEDINGS COURT AT

of

Applicant

of

Respondent

COUNTY COURT DIVISION OF

Order   [Appointment of a solicitor for a child
               Article 60(3) Children (Northern Ireland) Order 1995]

               Magistrates' Courts (Children (Northern Ireland) Order 1995) Rules
               (Northern Ireland) 1996; Rule 12

               [Refusal of the appointment of a solicitor]

               [Termination of the appointment of a solicitor]

The full name(s) of the child[ren]   Date(s) of birth

[The court is satisfied that the child[ren] [is] [are] not presently separately represented by a solicitor and

[● a guardian ad litem has not been appointed for the child[ren]; and]

[● the child[ren] [has] [have] sufficient understanding to instruct a solicitor and has expressed a wish to do so; and]

[● it would be in the interests of the child[ren] for [him] [her] [them] to be separately represented].

[The court orders that   [it refuses the appointment of a solicitor for the child[ren]]

                              [the appointment of]

                              [

                              of

                                                                                    ]

                              [be appointed as solicitor for the child[ren]]

                              [as solicitor for the child[ren] be terminated]

Ordered by

_____

         on

CHILDREN (NORTHERN IRELAND) ORDER 1995

FAMILY PROCEEDINGS COURT AT

of

Applicant   [PETTY SESSIONS DISTRICT OF]

of

Respondent

COUNTY COURT DIVISION OF

Order   [Transfer of proceedings to court]
The Children (Allocation of Proceedings) (Northern Ireland) Order 1996

The full name(s) of the child(ren)   Date(s) of birth

The court orders   that proceedings concerning the child[ren] be transferred to the

[High Court] [family care centre at] [county court]

because

The next [Hearing]
[Directions Appointment]
at that court   is on   at   [am]   [pm]

at

[will be advised by that court]

Please address all
future correspondence to

Ordered by

on

FORM C44

CHILDREN (NORTHERN IRELAND) ORDER 1995

[FAMILY PROCEEDINGS COURT AT]

of

Applicant   [PETTY SESSIONS DISTRICT OF]

of

Respondent

COUNTY COURT DIVISION OF

Certificate   Refusal to transfer proceedings

The Children (Allocation of Proceedings) (Northern Ireland) Order 1996

The full name(s) of the child[ren]   Date(s) of birth

The court refuses   an application to transfer proceedings in the case to

The applicant asked
for transfer on the
ground of
☐ exceptional gravity, importance or complexity
☐ consolidation

The court refused the
application [because]

Certified by

on

Note: An application may be made within 2 days for an order under Article 9 of the Allocation Order for the transfer of proceedings to a family care centre. The application should be made in accordance with rule 4.7 of the Family Proceedings Rules (Northern Ireland) 1996.

83

CHILDREN (NORTHERN IRELAND) ORDER 1995

FAMILY PROCEEDINGS COURT AT

of

Appellant

of

Respondent

COUNTY COURT DIVISION OF

TAKE NOTICE that I appeal to the above-named court under [Article 113] [Article 131(6)] [Article 145] of the Children (Northern Ireland) Order 1995 against the decision of   taken on

Signed   Appellant

Solicitor for Appellant

To the Respondent and to the Clerk of Petty Sessions

FORM C46

WRITTEN STATEMENT OF THE SUBSTANCE OF ORAL EVIDENCE TO BE ADDUCED AT [HEARING] [DIRECTIONS APPOINTMENT]

Rule 18 Magistrates' Courts (Children (Northern Ireland) Order 1995) Rules (Northern Ireland) 1996

---

of

       Applicant

of

       Respondent

In the matter of an application under the Children (Northern Ireland) Order 1995

This statement is made by
                   ("the maker")
on   day of   .
It is the maker's statement in these proceedings. The statement is filed on behalf of

I   declare that I believe this statement of   pages each signed by me is true and understand that it may be placed before the court.

Signed

Date

Notes: pages of statement should be on A4 size paper with a margin to the left. If statements are typed double-spacing should be used.

NOTICES AND RESPONDENTS

(i) *Provision under which proceedings brought*	(ii) *Minimum number of days prior to hearing or directions appointment for service under rule 4(2)*	(iii) *Respondents*	(iv) *Persons to whom notice is to be given*
All applications	See separate entries below	Subject to separate entries below: every person whom the applicant believes to have parental responsibility for the child; where the child is the subject of a care order, every person whom the applicant believes to have had parental responsibility immediately prior to the making of the care order; in the case of an application to extend, vary or discharge an order, the parties to the proceedings leading to the order which it is sought to have extended, varied or discharged; in the case of specified proceedings, the child.	Subject to separate entries below: any authority providing accommodation for the child; persons who are caring for the child at the time when the proceedings are commenced; in the case of proceedings brought in respect of a child who is alleged to be staying in a refuge which is certificated under Article 70(1) or (2), the person who is providing the refuge.
Article 7(1)(*a*), 7(4), 8, 13(1), 16(6), 33(1), 52(7), 159(1), 163(1) Schedule 1, Paragraphs 10(3) and 12(4) of Schedule 8	14 days	As for "all applications" above and: in the case of proceedings under Schedule 1, those persons whom the applicant believes to be interested in or affected by the proceedings;	As for "all applications" above, and: in the case of an application for an Article 8 order, every person whom applicant believes—

86

(i)	(ii)	(iii)	(iv)
Provision under which proceedings brought	*Minimum number of days prior to hearing or directions appointment for service under rule 4(2)*	*Respondents*	*Persons to whom notice is to be given*
		in the case of an application under paragraph 10(3)(*b*) or 12(4) of Schedule 8, any person, other than the child, named in the order or directions which it is sought to discharge or vary.	(i) to be named in a court order with respect to the same child, which has not ceased to have effect, (ii) to be a party to pending proceedings in respect of the same child, or (iii) to be a person with whom the child has lived for at least 3 years prior to the application, unless, in a case to which (i) or (ii) applies, the applicant believes that the court order or pending proceedings are not relevant to the application; in the case of an application under Article 33(1), the parties to the proceedings leading to the care order; in the case of an application under Article 159(1), the father of the child if he does not have parental responsibility.

87

(i) Provision under which proceedings brought	(ii) Minimum number of days prior to hearing or directions appointment for service under rule 4(2)	(iii) Respondents	(iv) Persons to whom notice is to be given
Article 55(1), 58(1), 58(2), 58(3), 58(4), 62(1), Paragraph 6(3) of Schedule 3, Paragraphs 5(2) and 7(1) of Schedule 4	7 days	As for "all applications" above, and: in the case of an application under Article 58(2) or (3), the supervisor; in the case of proceedings under paragraph 7(1) of Schedule 4, the education and library board concerned; in the case of proceedings under Article 55 or paragraph 5(2) or 7(1) of Schedule 4, the child.	As for "all applications" above, and: in the case of an application for an order under Article 62(1)— (i) every person whom the applicant believes to be a parent of the child, (ii) every person whom the applicant believes to be caring for the child, (iii) every person in whose favour a contact order is in force with respect to the child, and (iv) every person who is allowed to have contact with the child by virtue of an order under Article 53.
Article 50, 53(2), 53(3), 53(4), 53(9) or 57(8)(b)	3 days	As for "all applications" above, and: in the case of an application under Article 53, the person whose contact with the child is the subject of	As for "all applications" above, and: in the case of an application under Article 50—

88